History

A Guide to Advance

L. G. Brandon

Formerly Headmaster, King Edward's School, Aston

Edward Arnold

First published 1976
by Edward Arnold (Publishers) Ltd
41 Bedford Square, London WC1B 3DQ

Reprinted 1980

ISBN: 0 7131 0009 5

Printed in Great Britain by
SPOTTISWOODE BALLANTYNE LTD.
Colchester and London

Contents

Acknowledgments

The Publishers' thanks are due to Eyre and Spottiswoode and the author for permission to quote from *Henry VIII* by J. J. Scarisbrick, and to the Hutchinson Publishing Group Ltd for permission to quote from *Lloyd George: A Diary* by Frances Stevenson.

Introduction

We read history because we are interested in people and because we enjoy a good story. If the story is unusual or sensational we remember it easily, and feel quite resentful in later life when told that there is little evidence that Alfred burnt the cakes or that Drake said: 'There is time to finish the game and beat the Spaniards afterwards.'

For the early years of schooling history books are specially written with the purpose of describing events and people in clear and simple outline. It is not usual, at this stage, to ask how we know that the descriptions are accurate, but this question becomes increasingly important in later years. At sixth-form level and beyond history is still a treasure-house of fascinating stories, but it demands the skills of a detective and the careful study of the writings of professional historians. Their work is often clear but seldom simple.

The purpose of this book is to suggest some of the ways in which the serious study of history may be attempted.

A Historical evidence

Everything that we know about the past has been pieced together from evidence which has survived into the present. All this evidence has provided the clues, and historians and archaeologists have drawn inferences from them and suggested what they teach us. The clues seldom speak for themselves: they need the interpretation of experts. When the foundations of a Roman building are uncovered, the tourist may see only trenches and rubble: the archaeologist can suggest the likely shape of the completed structure and the probable purpose for which it was built.

Historical evidence appears in a multitude of different forms. These are some of the most important:

(a) physical objects which were made or adapted by man. These include fields, hedges, roads, cottages, houses, city-walls, castles, churches, grave-stones, tools, furniture and clothing;

(b) documents concerning legal, domestic or business matters, produced for a thoroughly practical purpose at the time, with no thought that they would be eagerly read by historians. Examples are: contracts between business partners, legal deeds transferring property from one person to another, agreements to pay rent, lists of possessions in wills, assessments of income-tax or death-duties, and price-catalogues of goods offered for sale;
(c) more personal documents, such as letters or diaries, which were intended to be private;
(d) diaries and memoirs which the authors intended to publish;
(e) narratives of events in which the writers were concerned or interested.

These are some of the *primary sources* from which the historian extracts his clues. Normally he will work upon a closely restricted range of topics, because he regards it as his duty to study every relevant document which is known to exist. If he is denied access to part of the evidence, he knows that his study will be incomplete. The author of a recent book *The Young Lloyd George* was not allowed to use documents in the possession of one member of the family; and all writers concerned with recent history are gravely handicapped by the fact that many official Government papers remain secret until many years after the events with which they were connected.

Historical research is the study of primary sources. When the results of the research are published, it is convenient to call the book a *monograph*, because it deals mainly with one major topic. If the work has been well done, other historians regard the new book as a *secondary source* which they will be prepared to use in their own studies. Scholarly research is such a complex operation that historians are obliged to rely heavily upon one another.

B General histories

Sixth-form studies make much use of general histories, written in considerable detail and covering most aspects of a fairly short period. An example is the *Oxford History of England*, which ranges from Roman times until 1945 in fifteen volumes, published between 1934 and 1965, and written by eminent historians. Each author could rely upon his own researches for part of his general history, but his major task was to blend the researches of others into an acceptable and convincing whole. His footnotes indicated the monographs which he had used.

Such histories play a valuable part in advanced study, because they deal with so many aspects of the story, but they are unlikely to quote much from primary sources or to become involved in many detailed arguments. If the study of history involved only the reproducing of a narrative of events, then one might envy the people whose memories are almost photographic and who have the ability to absorb long sequences of general history. But in fact, questions in an advanced history examination are most unlikely to ask for the simple telling of a story. A glance at almost any paper will show that the questions normally pose problems. They ask 'How far was A influenced by B?'; 'To what extent did X cause Y?'; 'Discuss (or 'Consider' or 'Comment upon') the view that the war of Z was primarily a commercial war'. Clearly the examiners expect candidates to be ready to present their opinions and to sustain an argument based upon remembered information. They are not mainly concerned with the sheer weight of facts which the candidates have brought into the examination room (a burden which they may shed shortly after). But they are concerned with the extent to which the candidates have understood what they have heard and read, with the way in which they have digested it, (seeing how people and events are linked together), and with their skill in using this well-considered information as evidence for or against a particular historical statement.

1 *This information is given about a book of general history:* 'First published 1957. Revised edition 1966. Reprinted 1967, 1968'. *Which of these dates is the most significant in deciding upon the usefulness of the book?*
2 *If essays are to give training in considering and presenting historical arguments, will it normally be better to prepare for the essay by reading part of a monograph, or part of a general history?*
3 *Look at the general history book which you are using and consider how you could discover which parts of the work are based upon the author's own researches.*

I

Knowledge and Understanding

A Active reading and understanding

Your history course will involve many lectures and discussions, but a very important factor in the success of your work will be your skill in reading books. There will be monographs in the library, and it is vital that you should consult these from time to time; but your daily companion is likely to be a general history. How should it be used? There are many possible answers, but here are some first suggestions:

(a) select a chapter or a section which deals with a particular topic and read it fairly quickly in order to form a general picture of the sequence of events and ideas;

(b) read the same part again, more slowly, and have two separate pages for notes. On one page put references to any ideas or words which you do not understand, and the names of any people about whom you know little.

On the other page give very brief notes about the sequence of events and about any statements which you regard as especially important. (Later sections will suggest other references which you may wish to include in these notes when you have become accustomed to critical reading);

(c) work carefully through your first page of notes, using the index of your text-book and any other available help, until you have found the necessary information.

Make a special point of consulting maps, looking for all the places mentioned in the text. Physical maps are especially useful, because they may well give evidence of why an army marched along a particular route, why boundaries were disputed, and why certain favoured areas aroused the greed of their neighbours.

Whenever possible, look at pictures and photographs, so that places become more than names in books;

(d) find an examination question which deals with your topic and sketch out a brief answer to it in note form.

These suggestions are based upon two important principles: that all serious reading should involve as much mental activity as possible, and that all information newly acquired should be used without delay in order that it may be digested.

Through discussion and active reading we aim to achieve an understanding of historical statements and ideas. We need to know what history is about, how historical information has been collected, and how historians have selected their evidence and compressed their conclusions.

The following sections attempt to illustrate some of the processes involved in the attempt to read history with understanding.

B The danger of having knowledge without understanding

In a limited sense, knowledge may exist without understanding: I may know what the book says, repeat it and gain a mark, and yet have no real grasp of the meaning of the words. I can state that Luther denied the doctrine of Transubstantiation, but if I cannot explain this doctrine my knowledge is entirely superficial. I may call Thomas Cromwell 'a tireless administrator', but if I cannot form a mental picture of the sorts of work which he tackled daily, and of the ways in which he did it, I am nothing but a parrot.

History is about people, not about sentences in history books. Our main objective should be to form clear mental pictures of people in action, but until we have the time and the opportunity to study primary sources in detail we are obliged to try to sketch out these pictures by studying the statements in general histories and monographs. This requires deliberate and continuous effort.

Consider these statements about Elizabeth I, taken from well-known books:

(a) She lived simply, worked hard, and ruled her household with rigid economy.
(b) She was both intellectually and emotionally cold.
(c) Her entire nature was saturated with artifice.

If you repeated these sentences in an essay you would appear to know some facts and opinions about Elizabeth, but what evidence could you give to back up the statements, and how far have they helped you to form a clearer picture of a remarkable woman?

Each statement about Elizabeth is *general* in form: that is, it covers a multitude of actions and attitudes known to the author, and denotes the general impression which they made upon him. For example, 'She lived simply' might be intended to convey the impression created by the following description, which came, indirectly, from somebody who knew Elizabeth:

> 'She ate very little, but then she chose what was pleasant and easy of digestion . . . she seldom drank above three times at a meal, and that was common beer; and she rarely drank again till supper. She would seldom drink any wine, for fear it should cloud her faculties: she loved Alicant wine above any other.'

This may have been what the historian had in mind: he was certainly not referring to her vast collection of dresses. But 'lived simply' tells us only that her living was simple in certain ways which are not specified. The author lacked the space to give us the details, and we must accept his general statement for the time being, making a mental note that we must look elsewhere for clues which will help us to form a meaningful picture which may or may not support his statement.

Sentences (b) and (c) are also general, with no vivid detail which suggests the actions and attitudes which the authors had in mind, and they are expressed in metaphorical language. This has its own dangers, which will be considered later.

In the three sentences historians have expressed conclusions reached after studying much evidence. If we repeat them, without looking for some of the evidence, we may show knowledge of a sort, but we shall not show understanding. It is only too easy to appear to show knowledge of history by stringing together phrases and sentences which have been remembered from books: but students who do this are not acquiring an understanding of people: they are thinking only about books.

Yet historical evidence is so vast in quantity that historians are obliged to pass on their thoughts about it in a greatly abbreviated form. The results of weeks of study may be compressed into a few sentences, and it is our business to be aware of this and to make ourselves familiar with the sorts of statements which historians find most useful. We may then discover how to make the best use of their statements.

4 *What metaphors are included in sentences (b) and (c) on page 5?*

5 *What evidence for or against statements (b) and (c) can be found in the following extracts?*

(a) From 'Queen Elizabeth's Progresses' by John Nichols. (Translation of the ending of the Queen's Latin speech at Cambridge University, 1564.)

'But now you see the difference between true learning, and an education not well retained. Of the one of which, you yourselves are all more than sufficient evidence; and of the other, I, too inconsiderately indeed, have made you all witnesses.

It is time then that your ears, which have been so long detained by this barbarous sort of an oration, should now be released from the pain of it.'

At this . . . all being marvellously astonished . . . spoke forth in open voice, 'Vivat Regina'. But the Queen's Majesty said on the other side . . . 'Taceat Regina' (Let the Queen be silent).

(b) A comment of Sir John Harrington, Elizabeth's godson.

. . . when she smiled it was pure sunshine, that every one did choose to bask in; but anon came a storm, from a sudden gathering of clouds, and the thunder fell, in wondrous manner, on all alike. I never did find greater show of understanding than she was blessed with . . .

(c) From the memoirs of Robert Cary, Earl of Monmouth, who had married in 1592 without the queen's consent, and had returned in 1593 after delivering a message to the king of Scotland.

I made all the haste I could to court . . . Dirty as I was, I came into the presence, where I found the lords and ladies dancing. The Queen was not there. My father went to the Queen, to let her know that I was returned. She willed him to take my message or letters, and bring them to her. He came for them; but I desired him to excuse me, for that which I had to say, either by word or by writing, I must deliver myself. . . . With much ado I was called for in: and I was left alone with her. Our first encounter was stormy and terrible, which I passed over with silence. After she had spoken her pleasure of me and my wife, I told her, that 'She herself was the fault of my marriage, and that if she had but graced me with the least of her favours, I had never left her or her court; and seeing she was the chief cause of my misfortune, I would never off my knees until I had kissed her hand, and obtained my pardon.' She was not displeased with my excuse, and before we parted we grew good friends.

C Some types of historical statements

The types are many. About each historical statement we need to ask: 'How can its truth be checked, and is it the sort of statement about which it can be said that it is certainly true, probably true, or only possibly true?'

Consider these extracts from *Henry VIII* by J. J. Scarisbrick:

> . . . in January 1536, Catherine of Aragon died(1) . . . By the summer of 1536, a time when Henry was riotously happy (2) celebrating his third marriage amidst incessant music, pageants and warm days on the river, there was grumbling unrest in the Midlands and North. In October it burst into rebellion. First in Lincolnshire, then in Yorkshire and the neighbouring counties, then in the North-West, there broke out a series of rebellions (3) collectively given the name the Pilgrimage of Grace—a title more properly confined to the outbreak in Yorkshire which began about 8 October and had Robert Aske as leader.
>
> The risings were so complex, were spring of so many different motives in any one area . . . as almost to defeat generalization. . . . In the North-West, in particular, economic and social grievances were predominant (4). Elsewhere landlordism, fiscalism and local politics played their part. . . . But when all this has been said and full allowance made for the way in which the risings were inevitably caught up in local and secular issues, exploited by adventurers who smelt easy loot, by victims of enclosure or rapacious landlords and so on, it may still be argued that the Lincolnshire rebellion and the Pilgrimage proper were first and foremost protests on behalf of the old order against the recent religious changes. . . (5). In short, it is difficult to rebut Aske's repeated assertion that even if other factors had not intervened, religious grievances (in the widest sense of that adjective) would have sufficed to generate rebellion. . . .
>
> I therefore support the contention of Professor Knowles . . . that the Pilgrimage was primarily a religious event (6), which, of course, is a long way from saying it was exclusively this.

Of the underlined passages, (1) is a simple statement of fact about one person; (2) is a statement about the emotional condition of one person; (3) refers to the actions of a large number of people; (4) lists the major motives for rebellion in an extensive area; (5) indicates that there is room for argument about the chief motives of the rebels; and (6) gives the author's judgment in this matter.

How can these statements be checked? About (1) and (3) there is no difficulty. The report of the chandler who embalmed Catherine's body still exists, and there is ample evidence about the incidents of the risings. For (2) Professor Scarisbrick gives no specific evidence—presumably he is relying on the impression given by Henry to the people who described the festivities. Is this conclusive?

(4) is a statement which could be checked only by extensive research into all that is known about the motives of the rebels of the North-West. (Such a study, by M.H. and R. Dodds, was published in 1915.)

(5) makes it plain that not all historians will agree about the relative importance of the various motives ascribed to the rebels, and (6) gives the author's own judgment, clearly indicating that it is an opinion, and not a statement of fact which could be confirmed beyond all reasonable doubt.

The study of these extracts was intended to show:

(a) that statements of facts about individuals may be the easiest to establish. (Though this is not always so. It is impossible to be certain about the year in which Thomas Wolsey or Francis Drake was born);
(b) that statements about the actions of groups of people are necessarily complicated. There was not *one* Pilgrimage of Grace, and a statement about one rebellion is not true about another;
(c) that descriptions of the thoughts and emotions of individuals or groups will usually involve an element of guess-work: that we *may* be certain about what people did, but that we can never be completely certain about why they did it;
(d) that historians give us opinions as well as facts. It is right that they should do so, because their judgments are based upon wide experience: but we must learn to recognise statements of opinion and not to confuse them with statements of fact. Later, we shall consider whether most statements about causes ought to be regarded as opinions.

If we take this investigation somewhat further, we may be able to decide that there are many other sorts of statements which historians commonly make; that they can be arranged in something like a logical order; that some can be rigidly checked while others can be no more than opinions; and that as we come to the end of the list we seem to be very far away from the real people and the actual events which started the whole process.

This is the process:

(a) *The event occurs* – an explosion, an earthquake, a sitting of Parliament, an assassination. From the outset we can be certain that we shall never know everything that could have been known about the event.

(b) *Observers* give the facts, as they know them or remember them, in oral or written reports.

(c) *Historians* study and compare the reports and then make statements about them.

Historians then combine these statements with others which they wish to make about a multitude of people and occurrences, and in their published works they write about:

1 *the actions of one person*. 'Asquith introduced the 1908 budget in person' (checked by reference to Hansard);

2 *the motives and attitudes of one person*. 'In cabinet he (Asquith) conceived his role as the chairmanship of a board, whose members it was his business to hold together by genial tact and judicious compromises. He was not the devotee of causes or ideals; he rarely looked far ahead; his concern was to carry on the king's government from day to day. (This is much more general. Parts could be checked by studying the reminiscences of Asquith's cabinet colleagues, or his letters);

3 *the actions of a group*. 'Three days later a very large force of Luddites, armed with muskets, pistols, axes and hammers, destroyed seventy frames at a large hosier's workshop in Sutton-in-Ashfield.' (This could be checked by reference to local newspapers, but details would be difficult to discover: for example, how many pistols?);

4 *the motives of a group*. 'Gladstone's first ministry was intent on abolishing privileges and extending opportunities.' (Did this apply to all the ministers, or only to those who were most influential, or whose departments were most closely concerned? Letters and memoirs of ministers would provide a check);

5 *comparisons of people*. (Of Castlereagh and Canning): 'The difference between their conduct of affairs was dictated by changing circumstances rather than by any fundamental conflict of principle.' (Evidence could be sought about their declared principles and about changing circumstances, but this is an announcement of the writer's opinion, and, as such, it can be supported or disputed but not proved or disproved);

6 *general trends in the community*. 'Between 1603 and 1640 the rich became richer and the poor, poorer.' (A very broad statement, with no indication of the limits of each group. A convincing check from statistical information might be very difficult);

7 *causes which link the actions of individuals and groups*. 'The rise and decline

of Chartism reflected changes in the economic climate.' (A very general linkage of the political actions and economic conditions of many groups and individuals. It could be shown to be plausible or unlikely, but it is not a statement which could be completely verified);

8 *results of actions or policies*. 'The economic and social consequences of the dissolution of the monasteries have been exaggerated.' (Many attempts have been made to assess these consequences, and there is a considerable body of evidence for some parts of the country. However, the verdict is likely to remain a matter of opinion);

9 *comparison of the results (or causes) of one set of events with the results, (or causes) of other sets*. 'The motor-car was the greatest single factor in transforming social life in Britain during the period 1906–39.' (There is evidence concerning the social effects of the invention of the motor-car, and concerning the effects of other inventions, but they cannot be balanced accurately, one against the other);

10 *judgments about the abilities and achievements of individuals or groups*. 'Mussolini completely failed to solve Italy's problems.' (All such judgments are matters of opinion. The word 'achievement' usually implies that what was done was worth doing, and there will never be complete agreement about which actions improve the general welfare of a country and which do not);

11 *judgments about the morality of actions*. (Of 'Peterloo'): 'the panic was not . . . the panic of bad horsemen hemmed in by a crowd. It was the panic of class hatred.' (Again, an opinion strongly held, but not necessarily acceptable to other historians);

12 *judgments about the moral verdicts of historians*. 'I exhort you . . . to try others by the final maxim that governs your own lives.' (The words were spoken by Lord Acton. He believed that the best moral standards of his own day should be applied to all historical figures of the Christian era, so that if robbery on the high seas is wrong today, it was equally wrong in the days of Drake. But many historians argue that a man should be judged by the standards of his own day. The debate continues);

13 *general principles concerning human behaviour*. 'Revolutions occur only when conditions have already begun to improve.' (Evidence can be produced in favour of this sweeping generalisation, but many historians would argue that the study of history does not lead to the formulation of principles which are valid at all times and in all places);

14 *opinions which are expressed in completely abstract language* (see page 14). 'The Luddism of Lancashire revealed the highest political content, as

well as the greatest spontaneity and confusion.'

We have come a long way from the mental picture of armed men destroying stocking-frames by night, but we are not very far from the mental operations demanded by advanced history questions. Half the passages quoted above were used in recent papers, and they need to be fully understood before they can be discussed or commented upon in an essay-type answer. This reinforces the need for training in *critical* reading. It was suggested on page 5 that the most effective reading is always an active process. It is now recommended that *from time to time* you should study one or two pages in depth, looking for the people behind the general remarks, deciding what sorts of statements have been made, and how they might be checked, and identifying the author's opinions. Obviously this can be only an occasional exercise, but it has great value.

6 *Read the following extract critically and decide:*
  (a) what statements of fact are made?
  (b) how could these be checked?
  (c) what statements are made about mental attitudes?
  (d) what opinions are stated?

From *Henry VIII* by J. J. Scarisbrick:

The king was saved not so much by the loyalty of his friends as by the loyalty of the rebels. Time and again Aske refused to take advantage of his opponents' weakness and held back the hotheads who wanted to march boldly southwards and conquer, as they might have done, insisting that he and his followers were pilgrims, not rebels, come to plead with the king, not to bury him. Aske was Henry's most loyal, as well as his most critical, subject, and it was his integrity, his simple confidence that Henry would hear their petition, his faith that the king would not break his word nor wreak bloody revenge which really defeated the Pilgrimage.

2

The Language of Historical Discussion

Historians often pack the results of extensive research into a small space, helped by the use of words and phrases which convey their meaning in a highly compressed form. They use:
(a) technical terms, with precise meanings;
(b) general terms, which are less precise;
(c) group names, period names, and 'movement' names.

A Technical terms

These are liable to occur on every page. Examples are: 'freemen', 'villeins', 'leaseholders', 'copyholders', 'enclosures', 'petty sessions', 'assizes', 'rector', 'vicar', 'deacon', 'priest', 'advowson', 'regular clergy', 'legate', 'province', 'Convocation'.

A good dictionary will give the exact meaning of most technical terms, and further help can be found by using the index of a general history book. There are two important warnings: (i) beware of using terms which you understand only partially: (ii) be on your guard against technical words which have changed their meaning. Thus, a deacon in the Anglican Church is in holy orders and is likely to become a priest, whereas a deacon in a Nonconformist Church is a layman with duties which are thought to be similar to those of deacons in the Early Christian Church (see Paul's *First Letter to Timothy*, chapter 2).

B General historical terms

This is a convenient name for nouns, adjectives and phrases which refer to a background of historical information but are not often strictly defined. In the extract on page 8 Professor Scarisbrick wrote of *landlordism* and *fiscalism*, words which were probably intended to make us think of the many different types of grievances which might arise from the greed of landlords and the demands of tax-collectors. To be certain of this we would need to discover whether the words had been used elsewhere in a context which made their meanings completely clear. Unfortunately, they do not appear in the index to *Henry VIII*.

Many general terms are used constantly in historical writing. Examples are: 'feudalism', 'capitalism', 'imperialism', 'socialism', 'communism', 'absolutism', 'despotism', 'separatism', 'hegemony', 'administration', 'centralisation', 'bureaucratic', 'constitutional', 'totalitarian', 'reactionary', 'enlightened', 'democratic', 'conservative', 'liberal', 'radical'.

Most of these words are abstract in form: they do not stand for things which could be seen, heard or touched. We can picture Henry VIII ordering that Anne Boleyn shall be executed, to suit his personal plans, and we can call him a despot and say that any similar acts are acts of despotism. Despotism is an abstract general term, putting one label on to a number of different actions. We cannot see despotism, but when we read the word we can form mental pictures of the sorts of actions and attitudes it denotes.

Most general historical terms can have several shades of meaning, but they are extremely useful so long as we make the deliberate effort to look behind the words to the actions and attitudes which the author was thinking about. They are dangerous if we repeat them just as words from which we have formed no mental pictures. Here are two sentences which may sound quite impressive, but which were made up by stringing together several abstract general terms: 'In the sixteenth century feudalism played a steadily decreasing part in the organisation of English life. There were already signs that a capitalist economy was emerging, and the growing centralisation of administration was gradually diminishing the importance of feudal magnates.' These sentences are dead. I could bring them to life only by giving examples of what I denoted by the various general terms. (If this made-up passage seems to be exaggerated, consider this genuine extract from an important book. 'For this unity (of Church and Christendom) was not an inevitable and eternal condition, necessarily springing from the Church's own universalist claims; rather, it was the result of quite specific and transitory, even though long-term, historical conditions. These conditions were functional: the usefulness—not only religious but also intellectual, political, and administrative—of having both a universal faith and a universal organization which claimed to embody this faith.')

7 'The foreign policy of Elizabeth I, like her home policy, was entirely free from fanaticism.'

Explain what this means, without using the words 'policy' and 'fanaticism'.

8 *Consider these sentences about the Emperor Charles V.*

'When Charles V succeeded his father as Duke of Burgundy in 1506, he became a feudal overlord over . . . rich cities like Bruges and Ghent which had a long tradition of constitutional liberty. . . . Charles . . . tried to bring together the provinces under a more centralised administration, but he could not overcome their deep-rooted separatism.'

(a) *What sorts of privileges in their daily lives did the citizens of Bruges and Ghent probably regard as the most important parts of their constitutional liberty?*
(b) *What inconveniences might follow for them if the administration of the Netherland provinces became more centralised?*
(c) *How does a Scot or a Welshman of today show his desire for separatism?*

Pondering over the significance of words takes time, but most of the general terms used by historians are frequently repeated, and the mental picture formed on one occasion will probably serve very well on the next: and without this effort the words of your history book will not come alive for you.

9 *Looking for the precise meaning of words is extremely important in the examination room. Here is a question which demands careful thought before an answer is attempted.*
'Consider the view that Elizabeth's first great task was to settle religion.'
'Religion' is a much-used word, but what exactly does it mean in this context? Which of the following suggested meanings would you use in your answer?
(a) *Elizabeth's own beliefs about God.*
(b) *What English people were required to state as their belief about God.*
(c) *The forms of worship which would be made compulsory in English churches.*
(d) *The methods by which the English Church would be ordered and governed.*
(e) *The attitude which the Supreme Governor of the English Church would adopt towards the Pope.*
(f) *The obligation of English people to attend for regular worship in their parish churches.*

C Group names

Names used for groups of people may have different shades of meaning, so that we must study the context in order to decide which meaning is appropriate in a particular sentence. Consider the following:

Britain was not ready for war.
England retained the Ashes.
England was eliminated from the World Cup competition.
Germany had old age pensions before England.
The Asquith government introduced old age pensions in 1908.
Some ministers are members of the government but not of the cabinet.
He was a member of the working class.
The middle class in the counties were given more votes by the Reform Bill of 1867
The coal-miners decided to strike in 1974.

10 (a) *Explain the various meanings of 'England' in these sentences.*
(b) *Who actually introduced the pensions bill to the Commons in 1908?*
(c) *What is the precise meaning of 'middle class' in the sentence above? What other meanings does this group-name have?*

11 *Does the name 'coal-miners' indicate clearly:*
(a) *that it includes men who worked above ground?*
(b) *that the decision was taken by a ballot rather than by the union leaders?*

We need to realise that many group-names are not precise, and that failure to establish a particular meaning will lead to muddled thinking.

D Period names

'Classical Times', 'The Dark Ages', 'The Middle Ages', 'Modern Times', 'The Age of Reason', 'The Age of Revolutions'—these names have been composed solely for the convenience of historians and their readers. There is no correct answer to the question: 'When did the Middle Ages begin, and when did they end?'. Each historian is free to give his own dates for the years which he will call modern, but he will cause only confusion if his words suggest that there is a clear dividing line between one age and another. The fall of Constantinople in 1453 had important consequences, but it would be stupid to call 1452 medieval and 1454 modern.

It is also worth remembering that every man in every century has lived in times which were modern for him, and has worn clothes which only later generations have regarded as 'quaint'. William the Conqueror could not have answered any questions about the Middle Ages, or about feudalism, because he would not have known what the questions meant: but he had strong views about modern methods of castle-building.

12 *Suggest some appropriate names for the period of history since 1945.*

E The names of movements

'Renaissance', 'Reformation', 'Counter-Reformation', 'Industrial Revolution', 'French Revolution', 'Romantic Movement in literature', 'the Scramble for Africa'—these are all useful labels which suggest that highly complex events may be linked together to form certain patterns which deserve distinctive names. As with period names it is important to remember that these names have been given and preserved by historians because they help us to think about the past in an orderly way. There is room for many different opinions about the nature of the 'movements' and about which of their features are the most significant. Thus, historians will not agree about when the Industrial Revolution began in England, or about whether it has yet come to an end. 'Movements' have distinctive characteristics, but they cannot be precisely defined.

F Metaphorical language

13 *How would you convey the literal meaning of this description of Elizabeth I?*
'Circumstances had bred in her a hard, self-regarding type of mind, not particularly sensitive to fine issues, nor open in its acceptance of life, but strong in the grain and pliant as steel.'
How many different metaphors have you identified in this sentence?

Many historians have a great fondness for metaphors. Henry VIII was 'the pilot who weathered the storm', bringing the 'ship of state' safely home through the 'troubled waters' of the quarrel with the Pope. Wellington was the 'Iron Duke', and Lloyd George the 'Welsh Wizard'. Luther's beliefs were 'largely crystallized by political pressure'.

Metaphors make for lively reading, unless they have been used so often that they have lost all their freshness. We may be merely bored when we read that a politician 'kept to the straight and narrow path', 'explored every avenue', 'left no stone unturned', and 'restored the status quo'. These over-worked metaphors should be avoided in essays, and we are cheating a little if we repeat metaphorical expressions without fully understanding their literal meaning.

Appreciate metaphors, and use them by all means, but only when you are quite certain about the meanings which they are intended to convey.

Summary

Chapters 1 and 2 have suggested that the reading of history should always be an active operation, and that attempts should be made to form mental pictures from general statements, to become familiar with the various types of statement which are used and with the ways in which they may be checked, to study the compressed language of historians, learning the precise meaning of technical terms and practising the art of seeing people and actions behind words. It was also suggested that the nature of 'period' and 'movement' names should be fully understood.

If all the operations suggested in these sections were practised upon every page of a general history book, reading would be impossibly slow. Obviously there will be times when continuous reading is the most important need; but during such a spell it is all too easy for the mind to lose concentration; it will need to be pulled back into the activity of asking questions, and the previous sections have indicated some of the questions which may be useful.

Further help in the understanding of history can be given by the study of habits of thought (fixed ways of thinking about life) and by considering what historians mean by 'causes'.

3

Habits of Thought, 'Causes' and Prejudice

A Habits of Thought

14 *Consider the following statements about life at the present time, and decide: (a) Is each statement true? (b) Has it been proved to be true? (c) Is it an assumption, and part of your own habits of thought?*

A Deaths on the road are unavoidable.

B In a healthy society, the standard of living of all people will steadily improve: there will be more cars, more dishwashers, more colour television sets.

C The best guide to the efficiency of an industry is the percentage of profit which it makes on the capital invested.

D All people have the right to be fully educated at state expense.

E University students are best able to judge how their courses should be designed.

All groups of people, in all ages, have reached definite conclusions about the most important problems of life, and these have been accepted by the group as matters which cannot be questioned usefully. They have become habits of thought, involving assumptions which seem so obvious that they are very rarely doubted. The Jews of the time of Jesus were sure that they were God's chosen people, and that they could please him best by their careful observance of a number of intricate laws. Greek and medieval astronomers knew that all heavenly bodies must move in perfect circles. Medieval merchants assumed that all goods have a 'just price' which ought not to be exceeded. Sixteenth-century rulers took it for granted that only one form of religious worship could be safely permitted in a state. Most economists of the nineteenth century were convinced that the best way to help a community to become wealthy was to allow each member to achieve the greatest possible profit for himself.

It is easy to look back upon discarded habits of thought and to find them illogical and contradictory, but we cannot understand history until we realise that what we regard as old-fashioned and unacceptable was once as real and compelling in the minds of men as any of our own most treasured assumptions. We may have no use for the thought of eternal punishment, but we must try to imagine Luther's terror as he thought about Hell in order to understand the joy with which he seized upon the conviction that faith alone would save him from its horrors.

Habits of thought change very slowly. After Copernicus had given very strong reasons for believing that the earth was in orbit round the sun, it took fully 150 years for his ideas to be generally accepted. This is largely because most people feel very uncomfortable and often angry if their habits of thought are challenged. They have been brought up to believe that their assumptions are sound, and they feel insecure and unhappy if they think that they may lose any of them.

In order to strive after a full understanding of people of the past, we must try to see the world as they saw it, putting aside our own habits of thought.

We must always remember that we have the advantage of knowing what happened in the years after the events we are studying; that we may know that a statesman's decisions failed to achieve the results he intended. Neville Chamberlain's appeasement of Hitler did not avert war, but we have no right to label him incompetent because, in 1938, not knowing what we now know, he believed that war could be averted.

Also, we must guard against the temptation to belittle a way of thinking because it has been discarded in favour of another, which we prefer. We accept the modern Welfare State as an important factor in the relief of hardship, but we must also recognise the merit of the older view, which placed great value on independence, and assumed that it was the duty of every family to attend to the needs of all its members.

B Causes

It is natural and proper for an historian to consider how one man affected another, and how events in one place were linked with what happened elsewhere. In all our studies we are looking for relationships between events and ideas, and we feel successful when the material falls into an intelligible and plausible pattern. So the historian tells us what he considers to be the causes of the French Revolution, and if we are unwise we memorise them, without further thought, for use in the examination room. But when the historian writes that A caused B, he means that this is true *in all probability*.

A scientist can repeat an experiment time and again, until he can show that the truth of a particular proposition is so nearly certain, in the present state of knowledge, that it would be foolish to doubt it. But in historical investigations there can be no controlled experiments in the scientific sense: we cannot put back the clock and discover whether Henry VIII would have renounced the authority of the Pope if Catherine of Aragon had produced a healthy son. We can examine all the known evidence and decide that the lack of a son and the attractions of Anne Boleyn were very important aspects of the situation, but we cannot prove, beyond all reasonable doubt, that it was these considerations, and these alone, which caused Henry to act as he did.

Human beings and human relationships are so very complicated that there are always many possible motives for an action and many possible causes for an event. The historian selects the motives and the causes which seem to him to have had the greatest influence, but he knows that he is giving a well-judged opinion, not a statement of fact. Other historians, studying the same evidence, may well reach different conclusions, because each makes his own judgments about which parts of the evidence are the most important. One historian may stress political motives—the desire for responsibility and power; another, economic and social forces—the hunger for bigger cars, more splendid houses, and greater prestige. A third may think that the prime movers of history are men with emphatic beliefs and the determination to put them into practice. J. M. Keynes wrote: 'soon or late, it is ideas, not vested interests, which are dangerous for good or evil.'

New documents may be discovered or made available for study, so that a fresh assessment of causes becomes necessary; and new experiences, may give historians a deeper understanding of the past. Thus, an historian of the 1970s, made vividly aware of the nature of terrorist activities in Ireland, may feel that the Irish troubles of the time of Gladstone or Lloyd George now come alive for him in a new way.

For these reasons we must expect that assessments of motives, causes and results will be more likely to vary from book to book and from time to time than statements about basic facts. There is still no general agreement about the causes of the 1914–18 war.

C Recognising prejudice

The Joint Matriculation Board states that one of the objectives of its Advanced level history examinations is to test the ability of candidates 'to evaluate opinions and to recognise prejudice'. We are more likely to find prejudice in monographs than in general histories, though some of these give an openly Protestant or Catholic interpretation of British or European history. Opinions appear freely in all books, and when we have identified them we can test their value by considering the evidence which is produced to support them. In the light of this we can decide whether the opinion is probably correct, possibly correct, clearly doubtful, or clearly wrong. If no evidence is given, we must suspend judgment: but if the writer is one for whose accuracy, wisdom and fairness we have a high regard, we may sensibly decide to accept the opinion for the time being.

Prejudice often makes its presence plain by the nature of the words used by the writer. If an action is called 'foolhardy' it is condemned: if 'courageous', approved. The politician whom his friends call 'tenacious' is labelled 'stubborn' by his opponents. In prejudiced writing Communists are 'Reds', Conservatives 'exploit' workers, Labour leaders 'pander' to the wishes of trade unions, and the 'proletariat' are repressed by corrupt 'bourgeois bureaucrats'.

Words which, by their very nature, show how a writer feels about a subject are often called 'coloured' terms, because they colour or distort an account. The reading of history would lose some of its attraction if writers took great pains to conceal their feelings at all times, and little harm is done by a prejudiced account when once its bias has been recognised. Therefore it is useful, in advance, to consider what sorts of bias are to be expected in the books or documents which you study. It is important to realise that prejudice can operate effectively without requiring the writer to make false statements or to use coloured terms. Since there is always far more evidence than can be quoted in an account of appropriate length, historians are obliged to select part of it only. Unless they are constantly on their guard, what they select will be the evidence which supports a view with which they have strong sympathy. For example, many historians have believed that Britain's greatest achievement has been the gradual development of rule by a democratic Parliament. They have regarded any incidents which diminished the power of the King and increased the power of Parliament as important steps in the march of progress, and they have tended to emphasise them unduly. An important study of this subtle prejudice was written by Professor H. Butterfield, with the title *The Whig Interpretation of History*.

The effect of selection is just as important in the presentation of historical material in television programmes. A recent biographical picture of

Henry Ford used many extracts from news-films made in his lifetime, but because there was so much that was *not* shown, the selection may have given a false impression. Television 'documentaries' appear to be authentic and accurate, but there may have been scenes which the cameraman was not allowed to photograph, and permission to take the film may have been granted only on condition that the people concerned had the right to censor any parts which they thought damaging to their reputations. It is also plain that a news picture of a student demonstration, for example, is not good evidence of what would have happened if the cameras had not been on the scene.

15 *Which of the following are coloured terms?*

hooliganism
turncoat
crowd
alcoholic drink
negro
agitator
mob
strong liquor
crusader
a convert
thrifty
starry-eyed
doctrinaire
nigger
healthy vigour
firmly based upon principles
generous
timid
resolute opposition
spendthrift
cautious
idealistic
miserly
wilful confrontation

16 *What sorts of bias would you expect to find in the following?*

(a) A Catholic history of the Reformation.
(b) A Communist history of the British Empire.
(c) A coal-miner's account of the General Strike of 1926.
(d) The memoirs of a statesman.
(e) Articles of impeachment (for example, against the Duke of Buckingham or against Warren Hastings)
(f) A funeral oration or obituary notice.
(g) A pupil's testimonial, written by his headmaster.

17 *Comment upon the language in which the leading article of* The Times *defended the newspaper on 22 April 1834. There had been a large demonstration in London on 21 April in favour of the six farm labourers of Tolpuddle who had been sentenced to transportation for seven years.*

'Once more,—we have been called enemies of the working classes; but by whom? By miscreants who cheat and prey upon them. We are too upright to be flatterers of the wealthy, and what honest man will dare charge us with having *ever* abandoned or betrayed the poor. . . . Who raised and directed the public spirit of England against the vile massacre of the manufacturing poor at Peterloo in 1819. . . .? Who would now open the poor man's eyes to the snares and treacheries which his mock friends are practising against him, who but this *Times* journal?—the object of every villain's vengeance, and of every slanderer's abuse. On such creatures we disdain to waste words—we despise and defy them.'

4
Aids to Learning

A Note-making

Note-making is a valuable exercise, but it may take up a great deal of time. It is therefore important to consider what sorts of notes are most appropriate when reading a general history book or a monograph.

(a) GENERAL HISTORIES

It was suggested in chapter 1(A) that during the second reading of a topic in a general history, two separate pages of notes should be made. The first page gives reminders about matters which must be investigated further: the second page gives a very brief outline of the sequence of events. From these second pages it is often possible to show how events were linked together by making a diagram. On page 26 is an example of a somewhat ambitious attempt which links together a considerable amount of information about the Reformation in England from 1529–59.

It is important to build up outline sequences of events, and you may well find that you can do this most usefully by constructing diagrams of your own design. Some people prefer to make a systematic précis of parts of a general history, but this is a laborious task which may not be worth the time which it takes.

Other useful notes on a general history can be made with a particular essay-topic or examination question in mind. The relevant information may be scattered over many pages of the book, and brief notes will link these references together as the basis for a written exercise.

(b) MONOGRAPHS

The same method is valid if you are consulting a monograph with a given question in mind. If you have time to read the whole of a monograph you will not want to make extensive notes upon it. Instead, having read the book you might ask yourself the following questions, and give the answers in brief notes:

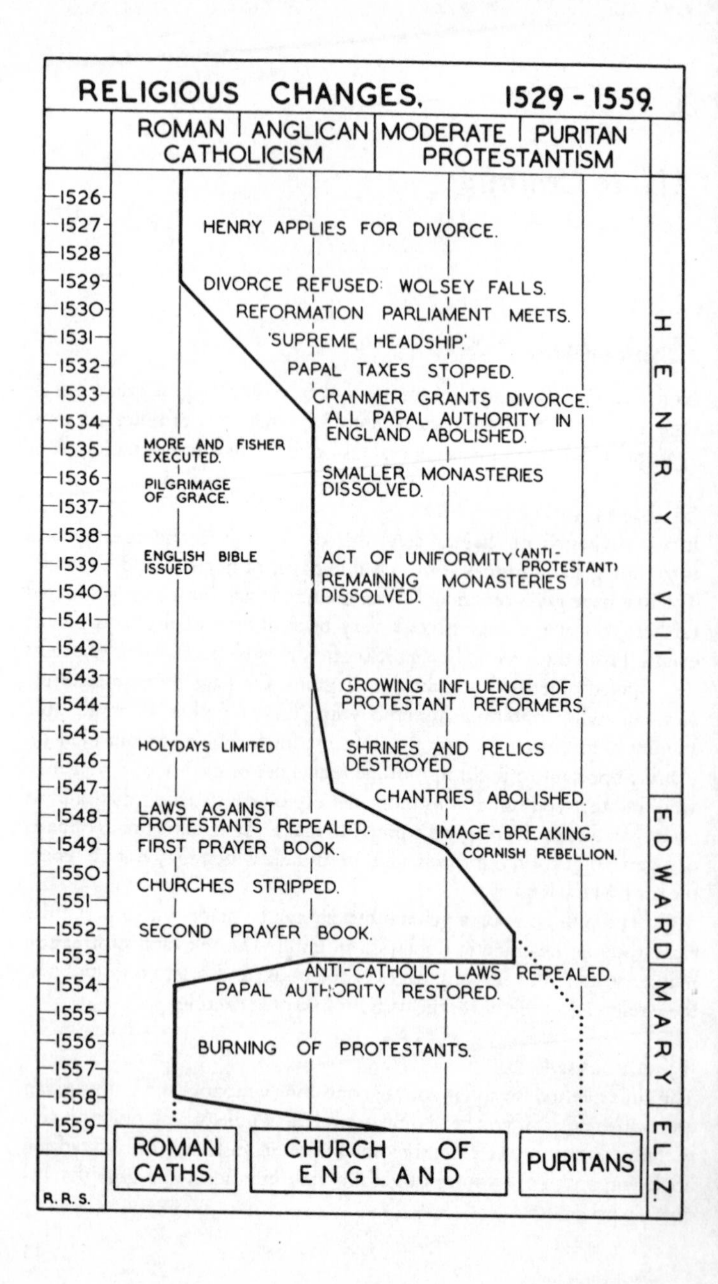
RELIGIOUS CHANGES. 1529 - 1559.
ROMAN
ANGLICAN
CATHOLICISM
MODERATE
PURITAN
PROTESTANTISM
1526
1527
1528
1529
1530
1531
1532
1533
1534
1535
1536
1537
1538
1539
1540
1541
1542
1543
1544
1545
1546
1547
1548
1549
1550
1551
1552
1553
1554
1555
1556
1557
1558
1559
HENRY APPLIES FOR DIVORCE.
DIVORCE REFUSED: WOLSEY FALLS.
REFORMATION PARLIAMENT MEETS.
'SUPREME HEADSHIP.'
PAPAL TAXES STOPPED.
CRANMER GRANTS DIVORCE.
ALL PAPAL AUTHORITY IN ENGLAND ABOLISHED.
MORE AND FISHER EXECUTED.
SMALLER MONASTERIES DISSOLVED.
PILGRIMAGE OF GRACE.
ENGLISH BIBLE ISSUED
ACT OF UNIFORMITY (ANTI-PROTESTANT)
REMAINING MONASTERIES DISSOLVED.
GROWING INFLUENCE OF PROTESTANT REFORMERS.
HOLYDAYS LIMITED
SHRINES AND RELICS DESTROYED
CHANTRIES ABOLISHED.
LAWS AGAINST PROTESTANTS REPEALED.
IMAGE-BREAKING.
FIRST PRAYER BOOK.
CORNISH REBELLION.
CHURCHES STRIPPED.
SECOND PRAYER BOOK.
ANTI-CATHOLIC LAWS REPEALED.
PAPAL AUTHORITY RESTORED.
BURNING OF PROTESTANTS.
ROMAN CATHS.
CHURCH OF ENGLAND
PURITANS
HENRY VIII
EDWARD
MARY
ELIZ.
R. R. S.

(a) What particular view of events is the author trying to justify?
(b) Does he appear to give ample evidence, and to select it fairly?
(c) Are his arguments clearly based upon the evidence, and are they convincing?
(d) Has he succeeded in what he set out to do?

This advice is based upon the assumption that you want to become more and more *critical* in your reading of history. As your skill as a student develops, your notes should become more personal, expressing your judgment upon the books you have read rather than summarising their contents.

B A card-index

There will always be some important facts which are difficult to remember because they are not part of a story or a sequence which hangs well together. In order to fix these in the memory a device is needed which ensures that the information is constantly revised until it is recalled with ease. A card-index is such a device.

Provide a number of small cards or pieces of stiff paper and on each write one piece of information. For example, if you find it difficult to remember that Herbert Asquith became Prime Minister in 1908, write on the front of the card 'Asquith's first ministry', and on the back '1908'. When you next look at the card, you can test your memory.

The cards should be kept in a box which also contains other cards labelled 'Week 1', 'Week 2', Week 3', 'Week 4' and so on. You then undertake a systematic programme of memorising. Your first cards go into 'Week 1', and by the end of the week you test your knowledge of all of them. A card with information which you cannot then remember goes into 'Week 2'; one of which you are certain goes into 'Week 4', or later. The others, of which you are *almost* certain go into 'Week 3'.

In 'Week 2' you will add new cards to those already filed under that label, and at the end of the week you will test yourself upon all the cards of the week, putting those on which you fail into 'Week 3', and so on. By continuing in this way week by week you will achieve constant revision, while spending most of your time on the facts which you find the most obstinate.

C Revision

Revision gives a natural opportunity to digest what you have read and to find out how much of it you have mastered. Before you leave the study of a particular topic you should always take a sheet of paper and write down brief answers to the questions:—What happened? Where? When? Why? With what results? This will show you the gaps in your knowledge and understanding while there is still ample time to refresh your memory.

Before an important examination it is essential to have a substantial period of special revision, and it helps greatly if this can be a time of mental activity instead of a depressing interlude of passive reading. The activity can be provided by the making of a new set of notes, of a different kind.

You know that there are a number of topics on which you will need last-minute revision in the days immediately before the examination. Therefore, if you begin to revise in ample time, you can make it your main business to prepare pages of skeleton notes which you will have time to study again in the final days. The effort of finding the best way to compress a lot of vital information into a small space will keep you wide awake during the revision weeks, and it will also help you to obtain a firmer understanding of the main themes of your period.

5

The study of documents

There has been a growing conviction in recent years that students of history should become acquainted with primary sources as soon as they can begin to understand them, and there is an obvious opportunity to study the works of man in town and country by visits to churches, castles, houses and museums. These most important sources of evidence are outside the scope of this book, which must confine itself to the discussion of some of the problems involved in the study of documents.

Many new volumes of documents for school and college use have now been published, and examining boards have introduced documentary extracts into their 'ordinary' and 'advanced' papers. For example, since 1965 the Joint Matriculation Board has set questions at 'advanced' level upon a number of documents which have been recommended for study, and also questions upon other primary material which the candidates are unlikely to have seen beforehand. These extracts have not been taken from documents which require highly specialised knowledge for their interpretation, and therefore they have included only the simplest examples of the material listed as group (b) on page 2. The 'prescribed' documents have included important statutes, but the 'unseen' extracts have come usually from diaries, memoirs and contemporary narratives. The declared objective is to test the candidate's 'understanding of the nature of historical evidence, and his ability to draw conclusions from this evidence.'

A Inferences

Drawing conclusions from evidence involves picking up clues and making inferences from them as detectives do, at least in fiction. Sherlock Holmes decided that an unknown criminal was not a Londoner because he used the spelling 'Edgeware Road'. Holmes' reasoning was:
(1) the unknown criminal does not know how to spell Edgware;
(2) all Londoners know how to spell Edgware;

(3) therefore he is not a Londoner.

His inference was based upon a sweeping assumption, and it is easy to show that his argument was unsound even though his conclusion happened to be true.

The clues selected by historians lead to probable conclusions only when they are interpreted by inference. For example, Sir Francis Drake's portrait, hanging in his own home, gave his age as 42 in 1581. From this it may be inferred that he was born in 1539, and the inference may be set out as follows:

(1) the portrait Drake saw frequently gave his age as 42 in 1581;
(2) Drake would not wish the painter to give his age wrongly;
(3) therefore Drake was born in 1539.

But the inference has involved an assumption. Perhaps Drake knew that the painter had made a mistake but did not bother to correct it. (A portrait of 1594 gave his age as 53, and other evidence suggested that he was born in 1544 or even later.) Whenever an inference has been made, it is always important to ask: 'Is it the only inference which is plausible?'

A modern birth certificate is taken as conclusive evidence of date of birth. Yet even this is an inference which depends upon the assumption that the parents of the baby gave the precisely correct date to the Registrar. Registrars occasionally make an independent check of the dates given, but normally they accept them as correct because it is very unlikely that the parents would have any motive for giving wrong information.

The bearing of this upon historical study is the indication that all historical evidence needs to be interpreted. The historian sets out to make its message clear, and he does this by drawing out inferences, which rest upon assumptions. If his assumptions are later shown to be faulty, he will need to revise his conclusions. From the violent outcry against Tudor enclosures, in sermons and pamphlets, it might be inferred that these enclosures were widespread and disastrous. But this conclusion rests on the assumption that the sermons and pamphlets gave a true picture of what was happening in very many parts of the country. When this assumption was shown to be very doubtful, the story of Tudor enclosures was rewritten.

The following pages try to suggest some of the routine questions which will help us to check inferences and to make good use of documentary material.

B Questions to ask about all documents

These are the first questions to ask about any document, whether of a personal, business or narrative type:

(1) Who wrote it? If it is unsigned, is there any evidence which enables the reader to make a probable guess about the author?
(2) When was it written, and where? If no date or place is given, are there any internal clues which help to solve the problem?
(3) What was its purpose?
(4) Who was intended to read it?

If the document is a narrative of events, or a description of people, we must obviously ask whether the writer saw what he tells us about, or had personal acquaintance with the people he describes. Beyond this, we will wish to know whether he was a reliable eye-witness and a perceptive observer of character. These matters will be discussed in more detail later.

Whatever we decide about the message of the document, our next task is to check our conclusions by referring to all the other relevant evidence which we can find.

C Internal evidence

It is often possible to answer questions about a document by interpreting clues contained within itself. Historians call such clues 'internal evidence'. Thus, it has been established beyond all reasonable doubt that the *Acts of the Apostles* had the same author as the Gospel ascribed to St Luke. This conclusion is based upon the opening words of *The Acts*: 'In the first part of my work, Theophilus, I wrote of all that Jesus did and taught . . .': upon the fact that both books show a particular interest in the preaching of Christianity to the Gentiles, and upon the knowledge that certain phrases and rare words appear in both books, but hardly at all in other parts of the New Testament.

18 *Here are two extracts from reported speeches. What internal evidence would enable you to suggest where each was made, and when?*

(a) I may remind your Lordships that in 1907 a Land Valuation Bill dealing with Scotland came before this House, and that your Lordships declined to pass it into law. The following year a similar

Bill came before you again. . . . Now your Lordships will observe that on both of those occasions this question of land valuation was presented to you as a matter with which you were perfectly competent to deal, and it does seem to me to be a thing unheard of, after that has taken place, that you should now be told that because a measure of precisely the same sort is grafted on to this Finance Bill you are to be deprived of the opportunity which, by common admission, was yours in 1907 and 1908.

(b) . . . it is absolutely inevitable that once salaries are paid to Members of Parliament who have control over the amount of their salaries, like all other classes who are paid wages, they will seek to raise those wages whenever they get the opportunity. . . . The Government . . . not content in this week . . . with destroying the legislative authority of the other House of Parliament, they are now proposing to destroy the moral authority of the House of Commons as well. It is because I love the House of Commons and am proud of it that I wish the votes of my hon. Friends on this side to save it, if possible, from this wanton and unnecessary humiliation.

When there is not enough internal evidence to suggest the probable date of a document, experts can often place it within certain limits of time by analysing paper and ink, and by studying the style of the handwriting and the special features of the phraseology. These, obviously, are highly technical investigations.

Even when a document is dated and signed, it does not follow that this evidence must be accepted without further thought. The writer may have given a false date deliberately, or he may have made a genuine mistake. Moreover, if he has writing before 1752, when our calendar was changed, his method of dating was different from ours. What he called 1 June we would call 12 June, and his New Year began on 25 March, so that 24 March 1700 was followed by 25 March 1701.

19 *Accuracy of date is of vital importance when a man is making his Last Will and Testament, and wills are sometimes forged for the benefit of unscrupulous people. If a man decides to make a will today without the help of a solicitor, he is likely to buy a specially printed form from a stationer. At the bottom of this form is a code number, which enables the printer to know when he prepared it and when he issued it to the shops. But if a member of the public asks the printer to decipher the code, he will refuse to do so. The information is strictly secret.*

(*a*) *If the code were not secret, what evidence would it give about the date of the making of a will?*

(*b*) *How does the secrecy help to guard against the falsification of wills?*

Signatures, also, must be treated with care, quite apart from the fact that they may be forged. The fact that a statesman signed a letter is no sort of proof that he composed it, even if it is in his own handwriting. The most that can be said is that he probably gave general approval to the contents, though he may have been too busy to make any alterations in detail. This applies, with equal force, to the letters of kings and queens. Unless there is clear evidence to the contrary, these are likely to be the work of private secretaries.

D The purpose of the document

It is reasonable to assume that all surviving documents were written for certain purposes. For legal and business documents the purpose is often obvious, and personal letters are usually a straightforward method of communicating thoughts from A to B, though some may be intended to deceive. But what of the letters which are written in the hope that they will be published at some time? Can these be regarded as sincere?

Why do people keep diaries and write memoirs, some leaving instructions that they must not be published, and others getting them into print as soon as they have a convenient opportunity?

In their value as historical evidence, is there a significant difference between memoirs which were intended for publication and those which were not?

20 *In September, 1916, Lloyd George visited the Somme battlefield, and on 21 September, 1916 he wrote to General Haig*:

'I can say, on behalf of my colleagues in the Cabinet as well as for myself, that the heartening news of the last few days has confirmed our anticipations and hopes that the tide has now definitely turned in our favour. . . . I hope you will let me come over to visit the scenes of your fresh triumphs.'

In his War Memoirs, *published between 1933 and 1936, Lloyd George wrote*:

'The whole mind of the western strategists was concentrated on one or other of the hamlets along the Somme. They were only waiting . . . for the final break of the German barrier. This is no exaggeration of their illusions. I saw them at this moment of exultation. . . . I traversed the front from Verdun to Ypres. . . . I visited General Haig at his Headquarters . . .

'The break through was postponed from victory to victory. We suffered enormous losses. . . . The Germans flaunted our wild onslaught on the Somme and advertised its failure by their Roumanian campaign.'

(a) *Did Lloyd George think in 1916 that the battle of the Somme was a 'wild onslaught'?*

(b) *In this extract from his Memoirs, does he imply that he did not share the illusions of the western strategists in 1916?*

In this context it is only fair to quote an earlier passage from the Memoirs:

'The Somme campaign certainly did not save Russia. That great country was being rapidly driven by the German guns towards the maelstrom of anarchy. You could even then hear the roar of the waters. That is, we might have heard it had it not been for the thunders of the Somme. This deafened our ears and obscured our vision so that we could not perceive the approaching catastrophe in Russia . . .'

Even if we assume that every writer of memoirs wishes only to tell the unvarnished truth, we must also assume that natural pride will make him reluctant to paint himself as a fool (though he may take perverse pleasure in showing himself to be a rogue). Therefore his view of the truth may easily become somewhat clouded, especially if he is writing many years later than the events he describes. Indeed, this frequent lapse of time must always be taken into consideration: and in this context it is vital to know whether the memoir-writer kept a daily diary during the years of his importance. If he did not, it is almost certain that he will make mistakes about details, even though his general picture may be as accurate as he is able to make it.

Some well-known stories about Elizabeth I come from the memoirs of Sir James Melville, who was Mary Stuart's ambassador at the English court. He wrote that in 1566, when Elizabeth heard that a son had been born to Mary, 'all her mirth was laid aside for that night', and that she complained 'that the Queen of Scots was Mother of a fair son, while she was but barren stock'. Yet the Spanish ambassador, who saw Melville on the following day, told Philip II that 'the Queen seemed very glad of the birth of the infant.'

Melville wrote his memoirs some thirty years later, and it seems very probable that his memory was at fault.

Historians use much caution in extracting evidence from memoirs, especially when they describe motives. It can be argued that a man best knows why he did what he did, but he may suggest in his memoirs that he carried out a deeply-laid plan when in fact he simply took advantage of unexpected events which worked out in his favour. The memoirs of Bismarck illustrate this tendency: A. J. P. Taylor made these comments on Bismarck's explanation of the 'Ems telegram' episode:

> 'Bismarck did not forge the king's message; he anticipated it. But, just as he had intended to blame William for any failure, now he would not allow him credit for any success. The edited "Ems telegram" was to be presented henceforth as the cause of the war. What is more, Bismarck was now eager to snatch the initiative from the French. This is the key to all his subsequent explanations. He had neither planned the war nor even foreseen it. But he claimed it as his own once it became inevitable. He wished to present himself as the creator of Germany, not as a man who had been mastered by events'.

21 *These extracts come from the diary of Frances Stevenson, who was Lloyd George's secretary, mistress, and, in 1943, his second wife. ('D' is Lloyd George.)*

November 22nd 1916
D. dined with me last night, very weary and preoccupied. He has a big scheme on now. He wants to get Carson back again to help in the conduct of the war. Carson says he is too tired, and is sick of the whole thing, but D. tells him it is his duty to come in and help him . . . .

November 23rd 1916
D. lunched today with Lord Derby, and Sir Douglas Haig and Lord Cavan were present. D. said he talked to Haig as a father to a child, and as he has never been talked to before. D. said Haig listened to him all the more because he had seen D. fighting alone for the Army at the Cabinet this morning. But at lunch he gave Haig his frank opinion. He said that there was a feeling of uneasiness in the country about our

military operations. We have been talking of 'great victories' for the last few months, but in the end it only means that we have advanced five or six miles. We have been using up all our splendid men and our hoarded munitions, and what has it resulted in: six miles at the most. The people know that this is not victory.

(a) *How much of this information came from Miss Stevenson's direct knowledge?*
(b) *What evidence from the second extract has a bearing upon the opinions from the* War Memoirs *which were quoted on page 34?*

Diaries not intended for publication can be expected to give a more reliable account of motives and events (as they were understood at the time of writing), but a clear distinction must be made between matters of which the author had direct personal knowledge and other affairs which were known to him only through the evidence of other people.

E Information expressed in figures

22 *If a retailer buys a camera for £100 and sells it for £150, in what two ways can his rate of profit be expressed?*

23 *If the interest on a bank loan of £100 rises from £10 a year to £15, this could be called an increase of 5%. What other description of the percentage increase might be given?*

24 *If you had no means of checking the figures, which of these would you be prepared to accept as most probably valid?*
(a) *Trade figures produced by the Government to show how badly the Opposition had handled affairs while in power.*
(b) *Opposition statistics which indicate that the country's economic position is improving.*
(c) *Figures produced by the Trades Union Congress which indicate that wage-increases have had a marked effect upon the rate of inflation.*

We are accustomed today to receiving much information in statistical form—monthly totals of imports and exports, detailed analyses of the cost of living, total amounts spent on food, tobacco, alcohol and so on. Civil servants accumulate these figures, let computers handle the arithmetic, and then form estimates about probable trends which should influence future Government plans. Thus, calculations based upon birth-rate trends led to the conclusion in 1973–5 that the demand for teachers would decrease because there would be fewer children to educate. Therefore Colleges of Education were instructed to train fewer teachers. Yet some previous estimates used in the formation of policy have been seriously wrong. Why are figures not always reliable?

If we ask this question about the statistical information available for earlier centuries, the answers are obvious enough. Few attempts were made to count people or things accurately, and the machinery for doing so on an extensive scale just did not exist. Gregory King produced detailed estimates of population in 1688, and divided the people into social groups. An earlier attempt of the same kind had been made by Sir Thomas Wilson, who published his *State of England* in 1601. It contained sentences such as:

> 'There are to be accounted in England about the number of 500 Knights . . . these for the most part are men for living betwixt 1,000 and 2,000 l. yearly . . .
>
> 'Those which we call Esquires are gentlemen whose ancestors are or have been Knights . . .; of these there are esteemed to be in England, as I have seen by the book of musters of every several shire, to the number of 16,000 or there about . . . these are men in living betwixt 1,000 and 500 l. rent . . .'

25 *What internal evidence is there concerning the source of Wilson's information and his opinion about its accuracy?*

Modern historians, and especially those mainly concerned with economic history, make great efforts to base their statements upon a solid foundation of statistical fact. They are not content with assertions that the conditions of life of the working classes improved or deteriorated between 1780 and 1850; they make detailed studies of all that they can discover about wages, retail prices, amounts of food consumed, purchases of other important articles, birth-rates, death-rates, and extent of unemployment. But because the statistical information is incomplete or open to varying interpretations, the results of extensive research by many historians may still be inconclusive. The position was summarised as follows (by A. J. Taylor, in *History*, volume XLV, 1960):

> 'Where so much remains legitimately controversial, the historian can at best draw only tentative conclusions. The evidence, however, would appear to permit two immediate generalizations. There is

reason to believe that after an early upsurge in living standards in the first stages of rapid industrialization, the pace of advance slackened, and decline may even have set in, by the beginning of the nineteenth century. It is also evident . . . that the progress of the working class lagged increasingly behind that of the nation at large.'

The detailed study of statistical documents demands very special technical skills: but there are some quite simple matters which we should consider whenever we deal with information which is expressed in figures:

(a) Are figures which appear to be precise intended only to convey a general impression? If an examiner gives a mark of 8/25 for an answer of candidate A, and 16/25 for an answer of candidate B, he does not mean that B's answer is exactly twice as good as A's. He is expressing his opinion that on this evidence B deserves a high grade and A does not deserve to pass.

(b) Do the figures relate to objects or ideas which are so well defined that we can be certain that each investigator counted precisely the same things? If the figures concern a man's weekly earnings, did he include payment for occasional overtime, or the value of free luncheon vouchers? Are all investigators working in the same way?

These considerations seem so obvious that it came as a great surprise to many people in the first weeks of 1974 when it was announced that the published wages of coal-miners had included items which were not counted in the wages of other industrial workers. Although this had long been known to officials, the disclosure created the impression that statisticians or other civil servants had made an elementary mistake, to the detriment of the miners, and much was heard of this during the February election campaign.

26 *What are the obvious questions to ask about the figures opposite, which were taken from a Board of Trade report concerning retail prices in industrial towns of the United Kingdom in 1912?*

Economic historians are no longer satisfied with general descriptive statements such as: 'In the period 1814–16 the agricultural industry passed suddenly from prosperity to extreme depression' (Ernle: *English Farming Past and Present*). They search for all relevant statistical information and study it in detail. The difficulties are many and the process is slow, but the results are likely to be more reliable than judgments based mainly upon the descriptions and narratives of contemporaries.

Predominant Retail Prices paid by the Working Classes in October 1912

Beef, per lb		Cheese, Canadian or	
British	8d–10d	American cheddar, per lb	8d–9d
Frozen	5½d–6½d	Butter	1s 3d–1s 4d
Mutton		Potatoes, per 7 lbs	3½d–4½d
British	8d–9½d	Flour, per 7 lbs	10d–11d
Frozen	4½d–5d	Bread, per 4 lbs	5½d–6d
Pork (British)	8½d–9½d	Milk, per quart	3½d–4d
Tea	1s 4d–1s 6d	Coal, per cwt	1s 0d–1s 3d
Sugar	2d–2½d		
Bacon	10d–11d		
Eggs, per 1s			
Irish	8–10		
Foreign	10–14		

F Contemporary narratives

Much use has been made of the important evidence given in Government 'Blue Books' recording the testimony of witnesses who were questioned during official enquiries into such matters as the conditions of work in nineteenth century factories or coal-mines. Also, for recent centuries there is an abundance of narratives, both printed and unpublished, which describe people and events of the author's own times. For all such evidence, the following questions are important:

(a) What is known about the author?

(b) When did he give or write his testimony, and where? Are there any reasons for supposing that he might not have been willing or able to tell the whole truth as he knew it?

(c) Which parts of his story concern matters which he observed for himself? From whom did he obtain the information for the other parts? How reliable were these other informants?

(d) Why was the narrative written, or the testimony given?

(e) Are we able to read the narrative in the form in which it was first written, or has it been edited and altered in any way?

(f) Does it seem that the author was a good observer, able to understand what he saw and heard? Did he record his impressions at the time? If not, is it likely that he would be able to remember the exact words of a conversation, or the precise sequence of a complicated series of events?

(g) Does the author show any clear prejudice for or against any of the people of whom he writes? If so, how would the prejudice be likely to affect his story?

(h) What did the author take for granted which seems strange to us? What seemed strange to the author and is taken for granted by us?

27 *In the autumn of 1580, on a date not certainly known, Francis Drake reached Plymouth after sailing round the world. The* Golden Hind *was laden with treasure taken from Spanish ships and settlements in South America, and the full value of the cargo is still not known, in spite of all the surviving evidence about the voyage.*

We have two accounts of the whole voyage and seven of parts of the voyage; all of them attributed to men who sailed with Drake. The following pieces of evidence are taken from these accounts. Consider each piece, and decide which of the questions listed above should be asked about the evidence you are studying.

(i) John Drake, a young cousin of Francis, returned safely from the voyage but was later captured by the Spaniards. Compelled to give evidence to the Inquisition at Lima, Peru, he stated in 1587 that his only share of the booty of the 1577-80 voyage was 'some articles of clothing'. *Does this prove that Francis had been mean?*

(ii) John Winter, captain of the *Elizabeth*, wrote that on 20 May 1578, Francis Drake, on the *Pelican* (later, *Golden Hind*), 'struck Thomas Doughty and bound him to the main mast.'

(iii) Thomas Doughty, an officer, was executed on 2 July 1578, after a trial. The accounts do not agree about the charges brought against him, but one story gives details of a heated argument at the trial between Drake and Doughty, and shows Drake as a thoroughly vindictive man who engineered the death of Doughty for his own selfish reasons.

The only known copy of this account is in the handwriting of John Stow, an Elizabethan historian. It is given as the story of John Cooke, and it is known that a man of that name sailed on the voyage.

(iv) The story of Doughty's trial and execution is often told in the words of a book called *The World Encompassed*, which was published in 1628 by Francis Drake's nephew. It does not mention Doughty's name, but states that a gentleman admitted that he had been involved in a plot to kill Drake and to ruin the expedition. He explains that he was offered a choice of punishment, but chose to be beheaded rather than to be set ashore or taken home in disgrace. A Communion service was held.

'The general himself communicated at this sacred ordinance, with this condemned penitent gentleman. . . . And after this holy repast they dined . . . each cheering up the other, and taking their leave, by drinking each to other, as if some journey only had been in hand. . . . Thus having by the worthy manner of his death . . . fully blotted out whatever stain his fault might seem to bring upon him; he left unto our fleet a lamentable example of a goodly gentleman, who in seeking advancement unfit for him, cast away himself . . .'

The title page of the book carries these words: 'Offered now at last to public view, both for the honour of the actor, but especially for the stirring up of heroic spirits to benefit their country, and eternize their names by like noble attempts.'

(v) In strict law, Drake had no authority to execute Doughty unless he was a naval captain, appointed by the queen and carrying her commission. Doughty challenged Drake to produce the commission. Drake did not do so, but maintained then and later that he did carry it. His assertion appears to be confirmed by a statement of a Spanish captain, Francisco de Zarate, who was Drake's prisoner for a few days. He said that Drake, talking about Doughty, had added 'that he had not been able to act otherwise, because this was what the Queen's service demanded. He showed me the commissions that he carried.'

Is this conclusive?

G The cross-checking of documentary evidence

Sometimes our knowledge of an event rests upon one document only. If the author is a man whose other evidence is known to be normally reliable, historians may be prepared to accept his story as probably true, provided it makes no serious clash with other knowledge which they have no reason to doubt.

A pamphlet published in 1624, when eye-witnesses may have been still alive, made the first known suggestion that when Plymouth heard that the Spanish Armada had been sighted, the 'Commanders and Captains were at bowls upon the Hoe of Plymouth.' A book published in 1736 repeated this sentence and added: 'and the tradition goes, that Drake would needs see the game up, but was soon prevailed to go and play at the Rubbers with the Spaniards.' Even here, it was not suggested that the game was finished, and the famous words: 'There is time to finish the game and beat the Spaniards afterwards' were put into Drake's mouth by later writers.

Here is a story which has been built up from the evidence of one pamphlet and from tradition. Historians ask, 'does it conflict with most of the other knowledge we have about Drake's character?' If not, it is at least plausible. Garrett Mattingly (in *The Defeat of the Spanish Armada*) goes on to consider evidence about the tides in Plymouth waters on the afternoon of 19 July, 1588, and decides that Drake would have known that it would be several hours before the English ships could leave the harbour safely: (in fact, they sailed soon after 10 p.m.). Assuming that the ships were fully prepared, there was a necessary time of waiting, and it *might have been* possible to finish the game without doing any damage to the prospect of success.

Thus, the original and scanty piece of evidence has been checked against other knowledge, and it is left to each of us to form our own conclusions.

28 *Which of the following statements do you consider to be:*
very probably true; possibly true; doubtful; almost certainly untrue?

(*a*) *The officers were playing bowls when they heard that the Armada had been sighted.*
(*b*) *Drake suggested that they should finish the game.*
(*c*) *The game was finished.*
(*d*) *This was done in order to show that Drake and the others had no fear of the Spaniards.*
(*e*) *The story has been gradually elaborated.*
(*f*) *The story is frequently repeated because it harmonises with the popular picture of Drake's cool and courageous temperament.*

When two or more accounts of the same episode are in rough agreement about certain parts of the story, the historian welcomes this corroboration. If they show almost complete agreement in detail, he becomes suspicious, and asks himself whether it is possible that one has been copied from the other. Thus, it is quite clear that *The World Encompassed* (see p. 41) was based upon three contemporary accounts of Drake's voyage, and that parts of two of these are identical in wording. Therefore, only those parts of *World Encompassed* which come from other sources can be of any help in checking these two accounts.

Sometimes it can be established that two accounts have been based upon a third which no longer exists. Bible scholars are agreed that the gospels of St Matthew and St Luke are based partly on St Mark, partly on independent sources, and partly on a lost collection of the sayings of Jesus which the scholars call 'Q'. Meticulous study of the contents of the gospels has enabled scholars to reconstruct 'Q' with some assurance, though there is still room for argument. In this way they make suggestions about the teaching of Jesus from a source which is earlier in date than any of the gospels. On this occasion historians have been helped by the fact that two writers used the same source.

As the historian cross-checks his evidence he confirms his opinion that some sources are strongly prejudiced, and sometimes this bias will yield a useful clue. A prejudiced writer will be unwilling to admit that the hero has faults, and such an admission carries great weight as evidence. Lloyd George's reputation is clearly affected by this entry from the diary of Frances Stevenson:

> '*July 26th 1916*
> The Irish negotiations have fallen through, and D. is depressed and worried about the situation. The Irish are angry with him: they think he should have upheld the original terms of the agreement, and I think they have reason to be angry. A large section of people think that D. should have resigned when he failed to carry those original terms in the Cabinet: he himself told me that he would do so if the Unionists refused them. . . . I don't think he has quite played the game, but on the other hand I feel that I must help him in every way that I can. . .'.

In a similar way, the praise of a man by his enemy is strong evidence of merit.

If, when all the checking has been done, the evidence yields no conclusion which can be shown to be almost certainly true, it is the duty of the historian to make this position clear by stating alternative conclusions and then indicating his *opinion* about which is the most convincing.

29 *Comment upon the following statement concerning Drake's voyage of 1577–80. It comes from a much-used general history.*

‘The truth is, Drake went forth with the queen’s authority to avenge the wrongs done to England by the Spaniard. . . . It would have surprised him had he been designated a pirate, for he had the royal commission to cover his enterprise. . .’.

6

Examinations

A Critical answers to essay-type questions

Questions in essay form ask candidates to think critically about their knowledge, practising their historical skills in considering a particular problem, selecting the evidence which is relevant, showing how it bears upon the problem, and suggesting a probable conclusion.

Unfortunately, far too many candidates misunderstand the position. Finding a question on a topic which appeals to them, they write a plain narrative of events, with no comments of their own. They show the examiner what they have remembered, but they ignore the problem set, and give no indication of their ability to understand historical material and to use it as evidence.

Examiners try very hard to show what they want by the careful wording of their questions. They rarely ask for simple narrative, and if they do, they almost always add: 'Describe *and account for* . . .'

Here is part of a paper set in 1972.

1 Assess the achievements of Thomas Wolsey as Lord Chancellor and in diplomacy.
2 'The person of the greatest virtue this kingdom ever produced.' Discuss this opinion of Thomas More.
3 Examine the ways in which Henry VIII exercised his supremacy over the Church in England.
4 What is the significance of Ket's revolt?
5 How far were England's relations with Scotland between 1540 and 1560 influenced by fear of France?
6 Illustrate and account for the deterioration in the lot of Roman Catholics during the reign of Elizabeth I.
7 What were the principles underlying Elizabethan social and economic legislation?

The danger facing the candidate is that, remembering previous essays and lecture notes, he will write down all that he knows about Thomas

Wolsey, Thomas More, Henry's breach with Rome, and so on, ignoring the key-words of the questions—'Assess', 'Discuss', 'Examine', 'significance', 'How far?', 'Account for', 'principles underlying'. The examiner has used these words with the express purpose of making his intentions clear, but he may have failed to do so. It is vital to decide exactly what his language means.

B The language of examiners

The examiner assumes that candidates have brought with them a useful stock of historical evidence. From that stock he wants them to select material which has a clear bearing upon problems concerning:

the aims of individuals or groups (motives and objectives: 'policies');
achievements—the realisation of aims and objectives;
the significance of the achievements. What effect, for good or for ill, did they have at the time, or later? By what standards has it been decided that they were good or ill?;
the causes and results of the actions of individuals or groups;
general assessments of the 'character' of an important person;
comparison of the character or achievements of one person with those of another;
comparison of the causes or results of one set of events with those of another set;
the nature of important 'movements' and trends (Renaissance, Reformation, Enlightenment; Industrial Revolution, and so on);
particular opinions, written by historians, upon any of these matters;
the process by which historians arrive at their knowledge and their judgments.

Each question indicates the topic to be treated and contains at least one guide word to denote the operation which is required.

(i) The most common guide words are very general—*'Discuss', 'Consider', 'Comment upon'*.

Candidates are free to express their own opinions and to make any observations which are appropriate to the main wording of the question. These general instructions may be assumed, normally, to indicate any of the operations which are discussed later. But if the topic is presented in the form of a quotation, it must be assumed that the passage has been chosen with the specific purpose of provoking a discussion upon each of its parts.

Thus, in question 2 on page 45, what is meant by 'virtue'? Is it the strict observance of Christian principles, the regular worship of God, the sympathetic control of family life, faithful obedience to the law of the land? With the meaning defined, what is the evidence about Thomas More's virtue? Has there been anybody else of 'this kingdom' whose virtue was greater? Were there any aspects of More's character which clearly destroyed his claim to supremacy?

Clearly, there is no one right answer to a question of this sort. It asks for the candidate's opinions, and he alone knows what they are. But he must show his ability by supporting them with good evidence and sound argument.

(ii) '*Explain*' is rather more definite. It means 'show that you have understood why things were as they were or happened as they did'. 'Explain the main differences between the teachings of Luther and the teachings of Calvin' sets a difficult task, because it involves not only knowing what the doctrines were but also understanding how each man came to assert his particular beliefs.

(iii) '*Examine*' strictly means 'test' or 'enquire into'. Therefore in question 3 on page 45 the candidate is required to recall examples of the ways in which Henry exercised the powers given to him by the Act of Supremacy, and to attempt to decide how far they were effective. The Act created or confirmed the legal position, but it would be fatal to answer the question merely by listing its provisions.

(iv) *'Assess', 'Estimate', 'To what extent?', 'How far?'*

'Assess' means 'to fix an amount' or 'to find the value of'. There is a clear indication that something is to be measured, even though the answer cannot be expressed in numbers.

The other three terms give the same guidance. The topic to be considered concerns achievements, influences or other matters which can vary widely in importance or amount. The candidate is asked to weigh up his evidence and to reach a conclusion which shows the significance of certain aspects of the topic.

Question 1 on page 45 concerns Wolsey as Lord Chancellor, and also as a diplomat. The answer to the first part involves knowledge of the duties of the Lord Chancellor and of the skill with which Wolsey performed them. The answer to the second part will outline the main objectives of Wolsey's dealings with European rulers and attempt to decide how far they were achieved. It will be relevant to decide whether what Wolsey did had any short or long-term value for the king, and, indirectly, for the country.

(v) *'Illustrate and account for', 'Trace and account for'*

These guide words are dangerous, because they ask for a descriptive statement, to be followed by a discussion of causes. There is a temptation for candidates to give a simple narrative account, and to ignore the second part of the question.

In question 6 on page 45 the 'deterioration' is taken for granted, and to 'illustrate' it will involve considering how Catholics were treated at the beginning of the reign, and how the penal laws imposed increasing restrictions. A comprehensive list of their provisions is not required, but it is appropriate to ask whether they were strictly enforced, and to produce relevant evidence.

To 'account for' the deterioration involves considering the probable motives of Elizabeth and her statesmen, and the changing political circumstances which formed the background to their decisions.

Other questions about causes are often obvious enough, but it is useful to remember that the answers almost certainly involve elements of opinion.

(vi) *'What is the significance of?'*

This invites consideration of the important consequences of a man's political, economic or artistic work. It suggests the questions: 'What did he do? What was its value?', 'How has the value been judged?', 'Who benefitted from it?'. It may also be used to ask for the results of actions and events, over a short or long period of time. In question 4 on page 45, 'significance' suggests two lines of thought: what can be learnt from Ket's revolt about conditions in his part of the country, and what consequences followed from the rebellion? The answer will consider the inferences which can be drawn about enclosures and other grievances of the time. It will also discuss the manner in which the rebellion was suppressed, the effect of the whole episode upon the reputation of the Duke of Somerset, and the light which it throws upon Tudor methods of government.

Thus, 'significance' includes not only results, but also any inferences which can be made from the evidence which is studied.

(vii) *'What were the principles underlying . . .?'*

Most candidates would prefer question 7 on page 45 to ask for a straightforward account of the Statute of Labour or of some of the Poor Laws. Instead they are asked to think about a whole series of Acts of Parliament and to decide whether they form any sort of pattern: whether they were based upon principles or convictions held by the statesmen who brought them before Parliament. These convictions might be about the importance of agriculture; about the need to restrict entry to certain crafts and to maintain high standards of workmanship; about the duty of the Government to see that the deserving poor were cared for in their own locality; and so on.

There is a danger that the answer will become overloaded with detail, and that there will not be enough emphasis upon the basic principles which seem to emerge.

(viii) '*Compare and contrast*' (the foreign policies of Castlereagh and Canning).

The instruction is clear enough. The important matter is to decide how the answer is to be arranged: whether to make the comparison step by step, or whether to deal first with Castlereagh and then with Canning, indicating the similarities and differences in some concluding paragraphs.

The first method is usually better, but the one thing to avoid is a mixture of the two patterns.

(ix) '*What were the problems facing*' (Elizabeth I on her accession?)

This demands careful thinking about the problems as they would be understood at the time, not as we have come to think about them since.

(x) '*What considerations influenced*' (Joseph Chamberlain's reaction to the Jameson raid?)

This means: 'Why did he act as he did after the raid?'. As a question about thoughts and motives it is very difficult to answer with assurance.

C A summary of advice

1. Answer the precise question which has been set. Assume that its words have been very carefully chosen.
2. Find out whether there are two or more parts to the question. If there are, assume that each part carries the same marks unless you are told otherwise.
3. Regard all your knowledge as important only because it can be used as evidence which is relevant to the solution of a problem.
4. Identify the problems in the question and spend time organising your evidence before you begin to write your answer. For example, if there are two or more problems, arrange your material so as to deal

with each in turn. Then, for each part of the answer, decide whether to give:

evidence in favour of point A — evidence against point A
evidence in favour of point B — evidence against point B

and so on, or whether to give:

all that supports A, B, C — all that goes against A, B, C

followed by paragraphs of comment.

5 Resist the temptation to add information which is not strictly relevant. It will not gain marks, particularly if it is a simple narrative of events. There may apppear to be a contradiction between this advice to put strict limits upon narrative and the earlier emphasis on the formation of mental pictures of people and events. What the examiner does not want is a stock story, given in laborious detail, and not relevant to the matter under discussion. But if, through reading with imagination, you have formed some striking impressions of your own, these are almost certain to please him.

6 Remember that what you write will be much more interesting if you form the habit of adding some colourful detail to illustrate (not prove) a general statement. For example: 'Drake endured hardship cheerfully, but he was fond of luxury. During his longest voyage he dined regularly from silver dishes and listened to the four musicians whom he carried on board.'

7 Avoid the habit, popular with some candidates, of memorising quotations from somewhat obscure books in order to give the impression that they have been diligently studied. It is not effective.

8 While it is useful, in a concluding paragraph, to make the message of your answer completely clear, take care that you do not merely repeat what you have written before. This wastes time and gains no extra marks.

9 Try to leave yourself time to read through each answer carefully. You may have made mistakes which you can easily recognise.

10 Above all, remember that a fairly brief answer, well reasoned and well set out, is worth much more than a long one, ill-organised, and padded with rambling thoughts.

D Questions on documents

Examination questions are set either on documents which have been prescribed for detailed study or on documents which candidates are unlikely to have seen before.

Questions on prescribed documents will assume that candidates are familiar with the historical situation in which the document was produced, and that they have a general picture of its contents (apart from the extracts which appear on the paper). They will assume that the wording has been carefully studied, and that all technical terms are understood.

Questions on 'unseens' will assume a general knowledge of the historical period, but not any detail about the background of the extracts. Uncommon technical terms will be explained, but candidates will be expected to understand the phraseology which was normally used in the period. Practice in reading contemporary documents is therefore very important. If the language is strange and the spelling archaic, it often helps to read the passage out loud, pronouncing the words exactly as they are spelt. A good dictionary is a necessary companion, and the editor's notes in your book of documents should be carefully studied. They will have been written with the express purpose of explaining obscure passages.

The purpose of all the questions is to test the understanding of historical evidence and the ability to draw conclusions from it. Obviously the tests may take a great variety of forms, but the following advice will always be valid:

(i) Read all the extracts with great care before attempting any answers.
(ii) Read the questions set upon the extracts and notice whether they appear to overlap in any way. It often happens that a candidate writes at length on question 1, and then finds that much of his answer would have been much more appropriate to a later question.

A recent question on unseen documents (which was quoted briefly on page 22) asked for the following skills:

(a) comprehension of somewhat difficult sixteenth-century prose, with the ability to pick out a sequence of events and to follow and reproduce the steps of an argument;
(b) the ability to find a number of clues, scattered over several pages, concerning the status and experience of the author;
(c) the using of internal evidence to establish the probable date of a document;
(d) the construction of a statistical table to arrange, in orderly form, the information given in the text concerning the numbers of men in certain social groups, with estimates of the average income of each group;
(e) recognition, from a careful study of the extracts, that a common word was being used with a special meaning.

30 *The word in question was 'ability'. Decide what it meant, using these key sentences:*

> 'I know many yeomen in divers Provinces in England which are able yearly to despend betwixt 3 or 5 hundred pound . . . yeomen of the richest sort which are able to lend the Queen money. . . . There are, moreover, . . . yeomen of meaner ability which are called Freeholders. . . . The rest are Copyholders and Cottagers, as they call them, . . . and these are some of them men of as great ability as any of the rest; and some poor . . .'.

It is quite usual for an examiner to ask for the detection of bias in a document and to give two or more accounts of the same events from primary or secondary sources, asking for the differences to be noticed, and perhaps explained. It is assumed that candidates have been encouraged to read with understanding, and that part of their practice has been upon documents of the period.

Some further advice can be given:

(i) If you are asked to explain the meaning of a passage, always do so in your own words. If you simply quote the words of the extract, the examiner cannot know whether you have understood them or not.

(ii) When you make a statement based on evidence in an extract, refer clearly to the sentences which you have in mind. Examiners may help you by numbering the lines of the extracts so as to make reference easy.

(iii) Follow the instructions precisely. If you are asked to give information in tabular form, be certain to do so. Give your answers briefly: essential information is required, not padding.

(iv) Since you will be expected to adopt a *critical* attitude towards the extracts, it is worth paying particular attention to the questions and thoughts suggested in chapter 5 B, E and F. Those in B and F might be remembered in the words:

Who, when, where, why, for whom?
How much seen, and how well?
How much bias?
How much altered?

Suggestions in E:

What was counted, by whom, from whom, and for whom?
Who prepared the result, and how was it presented?

7

Other types of examination

The writing of good essays demands very important skills, and it is likely that essay-questions will long continue to form part of advanced tests in history. Indeed, some examination boards are giving candidates the option of presenting long essays, prepared in their own time, and written upon subjects approved by the board.

A Objective tests

Some other modern experiments take a different direction: they attempt to frame questions in such a way that to each part there is one correct answer only, which must be selected by the candidate from several possible answers presented to him. All he has to do is to indicate the correct answer.

It is easy to see how this works when the purpose is simply to test a knowledge of facts:

King Edward VII died in

A 1909?
B 1910?
C 1908?
D 1911?
E 1912?

A series of 50 such questions, based, for example, on the period 1865–1914, would appear to give a fair test of factual knowledge, with the great advantage that the answers are clearly right or wrong, and that they can be marked by a computer.

The disadvantages are that the candidates are compelled to look at four pieces of false information for every piece which is correct, and that the examiner is bound to make a haphazard selection of 'facts'. Even if he resolved to select one fact from each year of the period, and to take it from a text-book which he knew to be in general use, he could not assume that the same fact would be stated in every other book on the period. Therefore his selection would be biassed in favour of certain candidates. The test is 'objective' because the marking does not depend in any way upon the personal decisions of the examiner, but clearly there is much scope for personal choice in the selection of the questions. This is one reason why such tests are tried out extensively before they are used officially.

Objective questions can test the ability to *think* about factual material, and many ingenious types have been devised. Some of these are not suitable for use with historical material. For example, the 'best answer' variety might lead to such a question as:

Of the following, which was the most important factor in causing Henry VIII to reject the authority of the Pope?

A His passionate desire for a son.
B His determination to be free to marry again.
C His infatuation with Anne Boleyn.
D His wish to be independent of all external power.
E His intention to possess monastery lands.

Clearly, it would be impossible to prove that any one of these motives was the overriding factor in Henry's decision. There is no 'best answer', and therefore the question is unsuitable.

A searching and ambitious type of question, used successfully for other subjects, could be constructed around historical statements which are clearly linked together.

ASSERTION AND REASON TEST

Instruction:

Consider the five assertions made below, and the reason given for each. Then, after each pair write:

A, if both assertion and reason are true statements and the reason is a correct explanation of the assertion; *or*

B, if both assertion and reason are true statements but the reason is NOT a correct explanation of the assertion; *or*

C, if the assertion is true but the reason is a false statement; *or*

D, if the assertion is false but the reason is a true statement; *or*

E, if both assertion and reason are false statements.

	Assertion		*Reason*
1	Acts of Parliament contain all the laws which the English must obey	**Because**	the Queen in Parliament is the supreme law-making body.

2	The Common Law is binding upon all Englishmen	**Because**	judges recognise its authority.
3	When judges interpret the law, their decisions become precedents to be followed on later occasions	**Because**	a law means what Parliament intended it to mean.
4	Judges do not depend upon the support of the Queen	**Because**	they can be dismissed only by the joint action of both Houses of Parliament.
5	All Cabinet ministers are members of the Privy Council	**Because**	they take an oath of allegiance to the Prime Minister.

Possible objections to this type of question are: that the candidate must not only work out the answers but must also master a code before he can give his answers correctly: and that he is obliged to look at false statements which may confuse him on another occasion. Perhaps this is not serious, but many people would be happier if efficient objective history tests could be constructed without making false statements. Here are some possible examples.

B Objective tests without false statements

1 A MATCHING TEST

Here are five statements concerning the work of government, followed by the names of eight groups of people who are involved in government.

After each statement, write the letter or letters of the group or groups involved in this part of the work of government.

Statements	
1 New laws are made	A Police
2 New laws are explained and brought into operation	B Parliament
	C Magistrates
3 A person who breaks a law, new or old, is identified and brought into court	D Civil servants
	E The sovereign
	F Government ministers
4 A decision is made about his guilt or innocence	G Judges
	H Juries

5 If guilty, he is punished in a way intended to make it unlikely that he will offend again, or that others will be encouraged to copy him

2 A TEST IN THE USE OF EVIDENCE

When was Sebastian Cabot born?

The date of birth of Sebastian Cabot is not known, but the following suggestions have been made:

A Not later than 1475
B 1480
C 1483
D 1486–7
E 1488

The following pieces of evidence have a bearing on the problem:

1 On 5 March, 1496, king Henry VII granted John Cabot and his three sons (including Sebastian) permission to sail to all parts of the world and to make discoveries in his name. It would be most unusual for such a grant to be made to anybody under the age of twenty-one.
2 On 31 December, 1536, Sebastian said in a lawsuit that he was 'fifty years of age and upwards'.
3 In April, 1538, a legal document stated in one place that Sebastian was aged about fifty, and in another, about fifty-eight.
4 In October, 1543, evidence in a lawsuit gave Sebastian's age as 'about sixty'.
5 Sebastian commanded a seafaring expedition in 1509.
6 In April, 1556, Sebastian was described as dancing at a banquet 'amongst the rest of the young and lusty company'.

Questions

(i) Which piece of evidence is best ignored?
(ii) Which dates appear to be ruled out by 1?
by 2?
by 4?
(iii) Which date is the most likely according to 5?
(iv) Which date is the least likely according to 6?

3 AN EXERCISE IN ESTABLISHING THE LOGICAL ORDER OF AN HISTORICAL ARGUMENT

The theory of indulgences in the sixteenth century

The theory rested upon the belief that sins are either venial (pardonable upon earth) or mortal.

The following statements give other steps in the argument. Place them in their correct order.

A Penance on earth will be ordered by the priest.

B The Pope is the guardian of the Treasury of Merit.

C If mortal sins are not confessed, the sinner cannot escape eternal damnation.

D The contrite sinner must still suffer 'temporal' punishment, on earth, in Purgatory, or both.

E Any mistakes made by the priest are covered by the Treasury of Merit, in which are stored the infinite good works of Christ, the Virgin Mary, and the Saints.

F A gift (indulgence) from the Treasury of Merit cancels all temporal punishment.

G If mortal sins are confessed to a priest, a contrite sinner receives absolution.

H The Pope can grant indulgences to reduce or cancel the pains of Purgatory.

I The priest may remit part of the earthly penance because of illness, or in return for almsgiving. But his calculations may be wrong, and he may have thought that the sinner was fully contrite when he was only partially so.

Having sorted out the steps of the argument, give the initial letter of step 3 and step 6.

This may be a difficult exercise, but it is intended to show that a searching test of understanding can be set and marked in an objective manner.

Index